Teacher Affirmations

Layout and typesetting: Ms. Mems

HEAD START

Early Learning

HeadStart Early Learning's mission is to support parents, teachers and children.

It takes a special type of person to dedicate their lives to the service of young children.
Teachers are very special and do not get the credit and respect they deserve.
We have developed this affirmation book for teachers to know they are not alone, feel connected, confident and supported on their journey, as they take stock of their emotions, and plan for a better response each day.
This book can act as a devotional or a journal.
The goal is for teachers to have an encouraging word to hold on to everyday.

Headstartng@gmail.com
www.hsearlylearning.com
Instagram: headstart_earlylearning

Teacher Affirmations
Day 1

I am an exceptional Teacher.

Don't ever forget who you are, why you decided to become a teacher and what you sacrificed to get here..

P/T Tips with Ms Mems

MY NOTES

DATE:

"ANYTHING WORTH HAVING TAKES TIME."

Teacher Affirmations
Day 2

I go above and beyond for my students.

What does going above and beyond look like to you? Make some notes.

MY NOTES

DATE:

"ANYTHING WORTH HAVING TAKES TIME."

Teacher Affirmations

Day 3

I am supporting the children in my classroom to thrive in life.
I will do my best everyday.

Have this goal at the back of your mind.
This is the reason we do what we do.

MY NOTES

DATE:

"ANYTHING WORTH HAVING TAKES TIME."

Teacher Affirmations
Day 4

I will keep learning and developing my skills.

MY NOTES

DATE:

"ANYTHING WORTH HAVING TAKES TIME."

TEACHER AFFIRMATIONS

DAY 5

I understand that every child is different and has different needs. I will observe to know what each child needs.

MY NOTES

DATE:

"ANYTHING WORTH HAVING TAKES TIME."

Teacher Affirmations

Day 6

I will endeavour to research the best approach for the diffeernt learning styles in my classroom.

MY NOTES

DATE:

"ANYTHING WORTH HAVING TAKES TIME."

Teacher Affirmations
Day 7

My communication is always calm, kind, clear and respectful.

P/T Tips with Ms Mems

MY NOTES

DATE:

"ANYTHING WORTH HAVING TAKES TIME."

Teacher Affirmations

Day 8

I stop myself from reacting but instead, I think about the best response for each child and I follow through consistently.

MY NOTES

DATE:

"ANYTHING WORTH HAVING TAKES TIME."

Teacher Affirmations
Day 9

I will take some time to check in
with myself today.
How am I feeling today?

P/T Tips with Ms Mems

MY NOTES

DATE:

"ANYTHING WORTH HAVING TAKES TIME."

Teacher Affirmations
Day 10

Today I will observe my patterns,
my triggers and my
mindset.

P/T Tips with Ms Mems

MY NOTES

DATE:

"ANYTHING WORTH HAVING TAKES TIME."

Teacher Affirmations
Day 11

Today I will show kindness to myself

MY NOTES

DATE:

"ANYTHING WORTH HAVING TAKES TIME."

TEACHER AFFIRMATIONS
DAY 12

Today I will slow down.
When I am triggered and loosing
my cool, I will pause
and think before I respond.

MY NOTES

DATE:

"ANYTHING WORTH HAVING TAKES TIME."

Teacher Affirmations

Day 13

When I am overwhelemed by the heaps of paperwork, I will remember why they are necessary.

Write down 2 reasons why the paperwork is necessary.

MY NOTES

DATE:

"ANYTHING WORTH HAVING TAKES TIME."

Teacher Affirmations
Day 14

I will rememeber to look after myself and take a break when I am experiencing burn out.

MY NOTES

DATE:

"ANYTHING WORTH HAVING TAKES TIME."

Teacher Affirmations
Day 15

I am growing and gaining wisdom daily.

MY NOTES

DATE:

"ANYTHING WORTH HAVING TAKES TIME."

Teacher Affirmations
Day 16

I will respond graciously to the children in my classroom.

MY NOTES

DATE:

"ANYTHING WORTH HAVING TAKES TIME."

Teacher Affirmations

Day 17

I will support the child who is struggling with their learning. I will find strategies to help them succeed.

P/T Tips with Ms Mems

MY NOTES

DATE:

"ANYTHING WORTH HAVING TAKES TIME."

Teacher Affirmations
Day 18

I will support the child who is struggling emotionally, i will find startegies to help them succeed.

P/T Tips with Ms Mems

MY NOTES

DATE:

"ANYTHING WORTH HAVING TAKES TIME."

Teacher Affirmations
Day 19

I will support the child who is struggling physically,
I will find strategies to help them succeed.

P/T Tips with Ms Mems

MY NOTES

DATE:

"ANYTHING WORTH HAVING TAKES TIME."

Teacher Affirmations
Day 20

I am constantly unlearning negative thought patterns and mindsets that do not serve the children in my classroom.

MY NOTES

DATE:

"ANYTHING WORTH HAVING TAKES TIME."

Teacher Affirmations

Day 21

The success of the children
in my classroom is
my ultimate goal and responsibility.

MY NOTES

DATE:

"ANYTHING WORTH HAVING TAKES TIME."

Teacher Affirmations
Day 22

I am patient with every child's learning and ability.
I will discover calming techniques to use when I am getting agitated.

MY NOTES

DATE:

"ANYTHING WORTH HAVING TAKES TIME."

Teacher Affirmations
Day 23

My classroom is fillied with future leaders in different areas.
I am supporting them as they grow into the graceful individuals that they will become.

MY NOTES

DATE:

"ANYTHING WORTH HAVING TAKES TIME."

Teacher Affirmations
Day 24

I love my job.
I enjoy what I do.
I will choose it again.

MY NOTES

DATE:

"ANYTHING WORTH HAVING TAKES TIME."

Teacher Affirmations

Day 25

I am unlearning old thought patterns that do not support the children and relearning new ways to support them.

P/T Tips with Ms Mems

MY NOTES

DATE:

"ANYTHING WORTH HAVING TAKES TIME."

Teacher Affirmations

Day 26

I am working daily to create a mindset that will help me thrive as a teacher.

MY NOTES

DATE:

"ANYTHING WORTH HAVING TAKES TIME."

Teacher Affirmations
Day 27

My classroom is full of superstars, including me.

MY NOTES

DATE:

"ANYTHING WORTH HAVING TAKES TIME."

Teacher Affirmations
Day 28

My classroom is filled with bright, intelligent, thoughtful, creative, kind, and loving individuals.

MY NOTES

DATE:

"ANYTHING WORTH HAVING TAKES TIME."

Teacher Affirmations
Day 29

I am constantly working on myself.
I am an exceptional teacher.

MY NOTES

DATE:

"ANYTHING WORTH HAVING TAKES TIME."

Teacher Affirmations

Day 30

I am learning to identify and
understand my triggers.
I go above and beyond
for my students.

MY NOTES

DATE:

"ANYTHING WORTH HAVING TAKES TIME."

Parent Affirmations

Day 31

I am learning the true definition of LOVE, in order to truly love the children in my classroom.
I am supporting them to thrive in life.

MY NOTES

DATE:

"ANYTHING WORTH HAVING TAKES TIME."

MY NOTES

DATE:

"ANYTHING WORTH HAVING TAKES TIME."

MY NOTES

DATE:

"ANYTHING WORTH HAVING TAKES TIME."

MY NOTES

DATE:

"ANYTHING WORTH HAVING TAKES TIME."

MY NOTES

DATE:

"ANYTHING WORTH HAVING TAKES TIME."

MY NOTES

DATE:

"ANYTHING WORTH HAVING TAKES TIME."

MY NOTES

DATE:

"ANYTHING WORTH HAVING TAKES TIME."

MY NOTES

DATE:

"ANYTHING WORTH HAVING TAKES TIME."

MY NOTES

DATE:

"ANYTHING WORTH HAVING TAKES TIME."

Printed in Great Britain
by Amazon

42887703R00046